famous per

famous persons we have known

poems

by

Richard Robbins

For Cindy —
Best of luck with your poems.
Richard Robbins
Seattle 10/14/2000

Eastern Washington University Press
Spokane, Washington 2000

Printed in the United States of America

Cover design by Scott Poole
Book Design by Joelean Copeland

Library of Congress Cataloging-in-Publication Data

Robbins, Richard.
Famous persons we have known / by Richard Robbins.
p. cm.
ISBN 0-910055-65-3 (alk. paper) – ISBN 0-910055-66-1 (pbk. : alk. paper)
I. Title.
PS3568.O232 F36 2000
811'.54–dc21

00-010370

for Keenan and Lewis

Table of Contents

1. famous persons we have known

Lon Chaney, Jr., at the Supermarket in Capistrano Beach 3
Dick 4
Roethke on Film 5
The Bulldog Edition of *The Los Angeles Times* 6
Coming Back to Life 7
Artists and Their Garages 9
George McGovern Campaign Rally, San Diego, 1972 11
Surfing Accident at Trestles Beach 15
Mansface 17
By Moonlight 19
Stagecoach 20
"To My Very Good Friend, [Signed] Jimmy Hoffa" 21
Rosary 22
On Not Introducing Myself to the Poet Laureate When We Both Shopped for Art at the Phillips Gallery, Salt Lake City 24
The High Lake Past the Field 27
Paparazzo 28
May on the Wintered-Over Ground 29
Crossing the Arctic Waste with Ana 30
Meditation 32

2. *views of table bay*

Douglas Islands 37
Skin Diving over the Shelf 38
Lake Bottom 39
Painted Rocks 40
Fire Ring 41
The Dock in Winter 42
Orchard, April 43
Lookout on Miller Point 44

3. *fraction hymns and sonnets out of town*

Shrinking 49
That Year 50
Georgic After an Argument 51
Stocking Rock Creek 52
Self-Guided Tour to Avalanche Lake 53
Two Days at Arch Cape 55
Essay on Rime 56
Man Burned for Spying 57
The Argument 58
Redwing 59
After Being Quiet for a Long Time 60
Violent Hours 61
On the Train Across America in 1902 63
Moon in Smoke, Teton Park 64
How November Comes 65
Sign 66
Pictures 67
Lockerbie 68
Confession 69
After the Miracle 70
Our Empty House 71
Demonstration 72
The Heavens 73
The Lunar Driver 75
Bread 76

1.

Famous Persons we have Known

Lon Chaney, Jr., at the Supermarket in Capistrano Beach

You'd see them now and then, on the fringe
of their stardom—Dick Van Dyke, for instance,
sober at last after his show dissolved.
Mostly they aged well, in chinos and golfer's tan,

not a mark out of the ordinary
except for the too-white teeth, or they carried
the torque of who they were and no longer were
in a kind of walking hammerlock—plain

Bob Denver eating steak in surgeon's garb
at the El Adobe. You'd wonder why
that woman in a fox stole walking her hound
could look at you once, all of 12 years old,

and convince you to be her grandson forever.
Did you recognize who cast the spells?
Would they someday reveal themselves
like the gray man behind you at checkout,

shuffling forward with all of us, quiet,
eyeing his eggs for cracks and counting his milk,
heaping bananas high against the night curse
of leg cramps? Just as the clerk turns our way,

he straightens up at the gum rack and growls,
paws half-raised and bared, and the eyes,
the terrible eyes wide and red and old
relaxing now into all our delight.

Dick

In every town I live she calls for him,
and he is always Dick. Until this week
the phone rings mainly late, my wife and I
already dreaming, her voice smoky
as the background bar. I hear laughing,
billiard balls kiss along the rail.
No, I am not forgetting anything.
No, I am not just back from the Navy.

In Corvallis, I come close to looking him up,
know now where he works, but then the reporter
knocks. My new son sleeps at the bright window.
No, I have not been charged with rape.
Last Friday, his chiropractor phones,
wondering why I am late. Someone
stunned to hear my voice asks for Lorraine.
It comes to me, finally, then the afternoon obit:

Dick dead at 42, a lung case,
never flush enough for his own number,
too shy of creditors. Or nothing like that,
a new Buddhist, glad for the quiet
without everyone calling. I would have
met him sometime, you see, asked why,
how he did it. All that drinking, those women,
how it all turns violent in the end. How the man

shadowing me all these years still lives
to threaten my mortgage, my life. Do I
fall into him now? Do I assume
his voice when the calls, as they must, begin again?
Will I recognize the others when I seek them out?
Will my normal home proceed in its orbit
even after I've left it, my wife and sons
abandoned for the dark cruise to Sitka?

Roethke on Film

Huge as blowpipes on the ferry deck
drifting toward the bay, he stared through rain
and the bear-weight of muscle and blood
around his bones. There to the south grew clouds,
and the Olympics grew through them, through snow
to a heaven of the gods of speech.
Out of thick sky, their children had fallen
in names around him: Juan de Fuca,
Point No Point, Seattle. The world grew children of sound.

Of course he postured for the camera. Toady
cinematographers poured him drink
after drink and asked him to stand by the hearth
long hours after it roared. He should have
set their bags on fire, *then* recited.
He should have read Jane's elegy from a burning
house—saw then who would stay until the end.
Oh, I know who cared about image more than most.
Crossing the Sound, the cigarette hung just right.

Let water turn, root invade new ground, let
self assume its totem self—all clumsy
bear of it—and let Roethke be praised.
On a near hill inside us, leave his body
face-up in rain. Visit the corpse
as it grows away from its parts, a quiet
musical digression, stench to stench, blood
to bone to powder down a river warbling
toward salt, the map chorused with names.

The Bulldog Edition of The Los Angeles Times

It would go the farthest away,
to Las Vegas by train, New York
by air and dawn. Downtown drunks
would read it first, a nickel flipped

to overgrown newsboys coursing
through bars, their day suddenly old
and only just arrived. Some
would move stool to booth, crowd box scores

from the east into red flickering
light. They'd curse the Dodger/Giant
game put to bed in the fifth.
Stars would fall all around, markets

opening backward from Tokyo
to Hong Kong to London. The green
hotel lobbies would rustle
dark, quiet floating down as the dream

unwound, one reader at a time,
in each deep leather chair.
Sun came up through a slow haze
burning that edge of continent.

Coming Back to Life

I never put much stock in Elvis
until he moved next door, keeping to himself
during daylight hours, slipping out
with raccoons and owls to buy pink
Cadillacs for anyone that moved him.
Plenty of neighbors put in calls

to 911 about the prowler, tall
in his tall hair and leather, *Like Elvis*
they might say, *but of course it wasn't him.*
Into the dark morning, each man talked himself
blue doubting the nagging memory of ten pink
Cadillacs gliding by, the moon just out

and he hadn't even been drinking. Out
to the porch each citizen had gone, tall
as his money could make him, the kids pink
in their beds, in their dreams of elephants Elvis
probably saw in Africa himself.
And then came the line of cars, and then him

driving the last one—deep in night-dark but him
all the same, a prisoner of sideburns, out
for the 3:00 a.m. tour. Talking to himself,
each man slunk to his bed then, made calls
to the police complaining of noise, of thug-like Elvises
slinking through the yards, ready to trample pink

rose, blue aster, marigold, phlox, cosmos pinker
than any Cadillac, and *While it wasn't him*
they would say, *still, it's not fair that Elvis*
or the guy under the mask, I mean, should be out

keeping people awake. And then each call
would end, and each man would hate himself

for the lie. One by one, they'd dream the King himself
crooned his forgiveness from Heaven, blessing lambs and pink
Cadillacs, ninety in a row, ten for each call.
In the morning, there'd be no sign of him
around the salmon-colored house. Out
in our driveways we'd find cars Elvis

might have driven himself if it was him
who lived here, pink in the sunshine, pink in life, out
of the shadow dying calls us toward, even the risen Elvis.

Artists and Their Garages

—for Brian Frink

She came home and he'd sealed-off window
and double door, the whippet twirling in daisies
as the saw cut a noisy square high up
for skylight. Ten days later, insulation
snug in its joists, he finished his first
small piece, those splatters a mad halo
when he pulled it off the white, white wall.

I know a woman who keeps her first violin
there, who likes to think of it breathing in
all that humidity night after summer night
among the creaking bats. She nearly
killed herself once, breathing in too much
in the locked Hyundai. Now that her heart's come back
she can almost make out which whispering
piece below zero is rafter,
which rosewood, making the spare duet.

And then there's the one who burned his poems
and hoses all at once. Or the one who,
just a girl, tried nailing her brother
to a cross. Used rope instead. Planted him
against leaning rake and scythe in a bag
of peat moss. Her brother's a Jesuit now.
She's gone into fabric and performance.

And there's the man who built his own
from scratch, drove in every nail, laid
each roof tile until his back caught fire,
framed the small and large doors. One thing always
led to the next: hot wire to siding
to shelves to the last paint out of the brush.
In the end, he eased the cars to their places.
He went indoors, down ancient, lonely stairs
to the basement where he began shaping something
useful, maybe beautiful, with his hands.

George McGovern Campaign Rally, San Diego, 1972

1.

An hour before speeches, Bruce Morton
sucks smoke with a vigor that explains
his caved-in look today. Three people deep
from the rope, it's hazy bright, Balboa Park,
a eucalyptus thicket away from the famous
ape and penguins too drugged
on zoo grunion, too fond of everyone
to miss Antarctica.

2.

Expect the faceless
Secret Service and they appear from under
a platform, around the giant spruce.
If wrens flirt or sing, they fast lose voice
to a crowd filling backward, loud
as an April creek, crowd first on picnic blankets
in the brightening light as fog
burns away, then standing, pissed off
as others stand in front of them, crowding,
crowding.

3.

It's California, after all,
where recreation often turns
somber, if only on a long drive home.
It's well before fish tacos and RollerBlades,

three months after Watergate, before
the end of denial. It's California, four years
after RFK was shot dead
in the middle of our teens, there are
that many of us here. When we all
tumble loud over stones in our heart,
when all of us, young and old, wonder why
we're here,

4.

the small men begin talking—it is
the year of small men—and we go on
without listening, clapping anyway,
tiny fish in us nosing into current.
We know

5.

the big man is near
when all the cameras point away toward a pulse
of squad cars. A giant crawl of suits
moves at us before it lets out
the candidate for handshakes three people away,
and the talk we came for begins,
and it is right in spite of hecklers
eighty yards back near grassy lanes where old men
play bocci.

6.

The lenses look at us
now. They map us. On the news tonight,
four will represent the river of face:
an ex-GI on one crutch,
a plumber (you can tell), a grandmother
holding her newest, and your poet
in olive drab jacket, hair past
his shoulder blades, locked in a posture
of inadvertent reverence,
looking up to the stage, believing
something, looking stupid
for Bruce.

7.

Twenty years later, it is, after all,
the memory of defeat. People I know
and think I know are getting shot: the poor
or dumb ones, the ones who made a deal
with some judge. The father-in-law
I won't know for six years, back from two tours,
probably sees me that evening and spits.
He says now Dan Rather, for all his on-site reports,
never left the officers' club in Da Nang.
Jim probably swears

8.

at the glass version
of me, at Dan and Tom—all the newswriting troops
who feel alive and hurting
but don't know shit. That's what he says:
We don't know shit. We're just pictures, thin as
targets, moving. When the screen goes black
we go the way of electric snow, back
into our haze and blur while real people
who shouldn't ask certain things, don't,
and those like me who want to ask,
don't either:

9.

Not when the bullets tumble home,
no, we should just shut the fuck up.
Not even if it's right, and all the people in
are crooks, no, we shouldn't march.
Or even stand here cheering for someone who might.
Or even look the way of cameras.
Or be anywhere in the middle of a crowd

10.

or the goddamned futile argument. Not when
he, or someone like him, brought me up.
Not as long as the roads are still open, the lights
still on, and meat's in the stores,
and your mother's not turned whore or lost
a thumb or breast to the sadist's knife.
Not as long as your sister has that shine
in her eye. Be happy you know nothing.

Surfing Accident at Trestles Beach

When James Arness fractured his skull, my mom
took all the names and numbers, she

got the son's autograph, an X-ray tech
laying that cracked head down.

Sand in his hair turned up as tangled stars
awaiting diagnosis. All

around his brain on the light table,
a universe held, the victim

conscious now in the next room, cracking jokes,
asking for Doc and Kitty. He reached

for my mom, faked hallucination.
He offered to sign his wrecked board,

snapped in half and fluttering over tide pools.
By the time the on-call came,

he'd recited Yeats and Robert Service,
lost his balance once, invited

everyone to his house, took those loose words
back, ordered ten Shakey's pizzas

for the crew. Near as ever after that,
Dodge City boiled up once a week,

and I watched for the lawman's cracks to show.
Would he kiss Chester

or take a bribe? Would he turn to gardening?

Instead I saw him cut and slice

through kelp beds of violence, free-falling
wave-tip to base in pursuit

of the cruel. He guarded home and gold,
bright beach of our dream. And so

it came to pass that tropical storms
arrived regularly

in Kansas. Pier timber rattled straighter
than train or slug toward bent palms

inside the Longbranch Saloon. I was too
young to understand, but these were

the early days of metaphor. It was
the end of the West as I knew it.

Mansface

—December. Green River, Wyoming

Like Cathedral Rock or Newspaper Wall,
it's a stretch to see what's in the name. From south
or east of town, from north before driving
through the double tunnel under Castle Rock,
you see nothing but cliff rubble

with a Christmas tree at the crown. Then finally
from the west it's clear as ever, and not calm
like sculpted heroes in the Black Hills,
or praying, like accidental Indian
maidens on ledges every 20 miles

in mountain country. No, the rock there
places him in the middle of some agony,
his face turned 45° upward, the nose
and forehead bony or warted, the mouth
wide open as if that fossil Scrooge,

limed with trona, coal, and sandstone,
suffered the worst after only one bad dream.

Shoshoni called the river *Seeds-ke-dee*
but left the cliff unnamed. Trappers passed it.
From where he set out in love of stone wall
and water, John Wesley Powell
couldn't have ignored that face chin-pointing him

toward Flaming Gorge. On a walkway
above the UP tracks, it's not hard to see

my great-grandfather, yard master in 1912,
looking up every now and then to see
the light had changed, and the face and its color

with the light, the way we notice those things
out West, then turn back to our work.

Now the rock names a street, liquor store,
realty, rental warehouse, civic group, beauty
academy, the high school annual.
And so, after time, what we name
names us. From age 4 onward, children

put Mansface in every
drawing of town—make it, because they must,
less threatening, more and more like
grandfather taking his afternoon nap.
Students make up legends

for the visiting poet to praise
and take back home. Every April, Mansface
captures winter in its throat: You can hear
the ice breaking. Mansface hides the last wolf
in its ear: All summer it hears news

all the animals know. It learns the future. Even now,
it's talking to us, it's saying No to what's coming.

By Moonlight

—Yellow Bay, Montana

If we paddled our eight canoes
to lake-center, then drifted, one boat turning
like a second hand, one rocking and rocking,

one pushed broadside to the perimeter
of an invisibly assembling star,
we would call out our stories in earnest

whispers. We wouldn't disturb sleepers on shore
with the baby fallen in the open
foundation, with the officer's badgering

on a street in Quito. In the near black
we'd call across the water, losing
our faces to word. It wouldn't matter, as the stories

set out to find us, who had told them.
Turning and weaving among each other,
what matters is the plum-colored

car and the letting go that afternoon
a cousin died, the twin that couldn't be yours,
but is, the miracle after miracle

keeping us afloat like the stories
that began with signatures before their
destination and necessity erased them.

Stagecoach

When Apaches drag their asses
on the borax flats, the black dime
still fattens in the Duke's right lung.
In the carpetbag, Churchill's gold
—good people's gold—jangles in dark
like the first day it fell away
from neighbor granite, like the day,

later, when that broken citizen
dives into 1939,
his last half-eagle tucked
for his widow in the vest. A chalk
man swims on the sidewalk for days.
Walking feet take their taste of him.
By the time the bugle charges,

the gambler has taken his slug,
Andy Devine slumps north, horses
cooling themselves now for Lordsburg,
law, and forgiveness. Geronimo
gallops back toward nature: cruel,
penniless, ruined for love, lead
in his chest bubbling like nitrate.

"To My Very Good Friend, [Signed] Jimmy Hoffa"

—my grandfather's photograph

After we put you in ground, your dead boss
smiled a week on my mantel: a brief
interior grotesque. I never confessed
my friends thought you crooked because of him.
Even when they found you old, on your knees
in bird-of-paradise and rose, your hand
meant the feigning shadow of sin to them,
the shears even more proof, dirty with land

you probably didn't earn. Were my house
an American cathedral, his face
outdoors and stone, draining floods from high slate,
he'd belong in his weird way, steering worse
ghosts back to Hell. But I grant him this peace
and bury the look, these concrete shoes an old hate.

Rosary

Now that my life connects five decades, I begin
to notice the homes of California
longing for their shade. I know why my grandfather
watered the silk fuchsia
months before he died. Pasqueflowers bloomed
next to rails taking him away from Greeley, 1903,
and today they ink the borrow pit
all along that straight
red road through western South Dakota.
I know why the Black Sox moved to Idaho, in penance

among Mormons. I know the West lives
inside me, waiting for gold to be put back.
Once upon a time, we blew the desert up, saved
the world, turned federal lake beds
to glass. Valleys creak there with the weight
of lizard. The Delamar Mountains
kill men off in all weather, regardless.
If I want the real story
I go to Boise, L.A., Chaco Canyon:
each afterimage

on a continuous,
disappearing rosary large as the map.
I know why the lightning bug, dead on a windshield,
pulses five minutes before going out.
I know lava rock, wind down the lee
of Sierra, a trout-packed stream,
the rose garden in Missoula, five Chinatowns,

the Huntington Beach Pier,
the Bob Marshall, the Great Bear, Elko, Boron,
a secret home of rare phlox. It's not

surprising now, the second time in two years,
I sit in Lesneski Funeral Home
racing through beads, letting go of the last grandparent.
"The Lord's Prayer" and "Ave Maria" play
just as before, and all
the oiled seascapes are Lesneski's own.
I multiply my scorn by 10,000
to arrive at the mortician's life,
his hidden-button, dot-to-dot kitsch,
his self-loathing. Pop's ear lobe flares out like a wing

I press in, wing flaring back again, and I go
outside to smell the air of San Clemente,
heavy with fog and salt. I know
life crawls from the ocean
even as I stand there, my family in tears
inside a house that lies about dying,
about a wave breaking. And I know
no one's to blame for not being good enough,
for being just average. We are walking ghost towns
making the point, and a whole

continent of towns glows inside us,
towns on a string seen from a plane, one that maps
the progress of leaving.

On Not Introducing Myself to the Poet Laureate When We Both Shopped for Art at Phillips Gallery, Salt Lake City

Alone most of the time, basement to ground floor
to attic, alone until each seller
hurried separately to attend us, I could have
said hello, given my name, told him who
I knew that he knew, that I'd just taught his work.

I remembered never hearing one good
word about him. That he seemed to relish
grinding blue-rinsed writers into sand
at conferences on the Oregon coast.
I remembered when I thought all artists

naturally pure, and later, that he
and a certain other poet—the one who elbowed
my ribs on his way to a bourbon—
didn't fit. I thought I remembered him
rich, and hated him for that. I mistrusted

the half-smile I'd seen in photos, the one
I saw that day glued to his face: Was it a Buddha
in him, or proud distance from the whole
city around us? Was it really
a wince? Was he composing on the spot?

Still, the rooms of the gallery spread out.
We had them all to ourselves. Our shoes
on the fir planks made bigger noises
than they deserved, and I remembered
seeing him read his dead-father poems

18 years ago in San Diego: By the hearth

in the small campus cottage,
he read the famous lines. Even there,
that smile. No eye contact. The soft voice
with its slight Canadian inflection.

I was 22.
That was the year Achebe, Rich, Snodgrass,
Mezey, Ashbery, Snyder, Creeley,
Levine, Stafford, Koch, Strand, and Levertov
all came to town to change my life.

We'd come a long way. When the hosts
took us into storage no bigger
than an office to look at more, I saw
what captured him that day: the reedy
watercolor landscapes, one by one,

abstract enough to let us
in to them, fields like his own famous field
filled with absence. For me, I saw more
red portraits by someone else.
Together in that space, I thought,

How many times in America
will two poets share the same small room
thinking to buy two paintings? It was another
way of thinking I didn't belong,
of asking who I was instead of the better

How am I? and What needs to be done?
I never pointed out the coincidence,
never found out if he even cared. Who
am I? I kept asking myself, still
irrelevant in the foreign territory of art.

Take a walk and you burn a burning question

to ash. I left the gallery without
leaving a name, drove anonymous
past three houses my grandfather lived in
before 1910,

saw paramedics bring a woman back
in Liberty Park, passed the homeless down
by the Rio Grande depot, ended up
on I-80 west to Saltair, the flooded
lakeshore resort. You can make too much

of not making chatter, or saying thank you,
or you can write a poem about it. You can head
straight for Evanston and hit Wyoming
head-on, stopping where sage still pushes up
out of snow, quivers a little

in the new wind. If you stop the car
the pronghorn antelope, with little or no
introduction, will watch you. Don't dare make more
of it than coincidence. They will not take
more meaning than you deserve.

The High Lake Past the Field

In the near-dawn moving across
blue flax and black, stitching near rocks
to gray rocking hillside, oak,

she gives herself back, atom by
atom, to her reassembly.
She reaches water and can walk.

Paparazzo

When Jackie swims nude off Knossos
I fix her black delta midair
between sky-haze and green, between art
and soft porn.
She is my quail, my sleek widow.

I bend the fact of that star's gray look
the day we tell him whose car
ran off a road.
These are not his eyes, either.
He plays back the head-on

into my flash, a reporter feeding him
details, and I see the sweat
go back into him. I wrap him around each bone.
The world five minutes ago:
that's where his eyes keep lagging.

I'm there when Wallenda falls
and the archduke lurches. The night Lennon dies,
I'm in the doorway changing rolls.
All I want is to catch a man breaking.
All I ever want is to beat the bullet home.

And when I touch certain women,
they live forever. They rise from their baths
in love with my two eyes, even when
their faces crack at opera or at Cannes.
They want someone who knows how to smooth

the failing dayshine even when
it's gone, when two bodies twist into sorry Ls
along some ditch in Monaco.

May on the Wintered-Over Ground

Automatic as the amen of chard
gone rhubarb-red to seed, he again sits
and again feels for the easing of knots
he bound himself with without his knowing
Amen to the small death strokes inside,
to their minority, to his more-than-
50-percent wanting to flourish
despite the strain easing more slowly now,

slow as whole days. On his knees in the garden,
he tears second-generation weeds from root
and willing earth. On the dark, unsure ground
where spirit grows its wheat, he kneels slowly
down. Stars do not come out inside the chest.
Work, love, song are the sound of the chemical
hoe and nighttime angel moving hill
to small spinach hill, preparing his yield.

Crossing the Arctic Waste with Ana

Now that we're dying, on our way to fame
wider than our skins will stretch, you need to know
I saw the stones give birth to you
where that waterfall, far south of us now,
fell from prairie to ravine. I saw you
take shape from the mist, nothing for a heart
at first—no brains or ankles, no eye
or attitude—but then the hands came to life
and the body of you around them,
and even then the way you leaned against
a shore oak, touching it like a wound
you'd come out of the earth to heal, told me
everything. Who are we to keep magic
from leaking into our lives? Your hands
in their birdish way careened through the air
over a hundred rough men's homes. Women
loved you, too, Ana, and not just for the bread
which was the bread of laughing and dance
and life but for the sight of you
coming inside us, tilting on your wing,
the wind of your passing alive in our guts
like a courage we could never lose.
You were more real than we deserved.

Even as our dogs give out and the bear
makes its mile-wide circle until we drop,
I match you glide for glide. We're getting close
to that place on the ice we can lie down
head-to-head, two points of a star, the length of us
one compass mark, the heavens drawing
its slow rings above us as we die. I'll
save for then the story that makes us
rescuers of the world. You can tell me yours

as flags of every expedition
rip in bluster at the top of the world.
Submarines run softly through the dark
beneath our boots, voices coming up
through lines no different than time.
And this, this is where we've been heading
all along. We're walking square
into the bare music of living, Ana.
The miracle of your hand points the way.

Meditation

She must begin without discerning who lit
today's candle or why the rose-headed
finches haven't yet come to feed. Too long ago
rain stopped falling firm, without quarrel,

through the airscape of her spirit. Fenceboards
rattle in their slats inside this new rain
not trying to drop, not intending
to wash or ruin, to have watchers find in it

pain or the end of pain, navies of slugs
moving out from beneath the home, the fence,
the pile of rusting cans. The heart swivels back
while a nearby floor draws in elm-and-tractor song

from outdoors. She is a candle of sound,
a field uncontaminated by the known.

2.

Views of Table Bay

— *for my grandparents*

Douglas Islands

A hundred yards off Miller Point,
just north of the big island, I pull
the throttle all the way
back to a crawl. The dead wake lifts beneath

me, heading alone toward mid-lake, and I let
shiny tackle catch and drop
in that quick glide left over from the
race out of Table Bay.

Years ago you showed me
around those two acres of fir and berry.
Thirty years ago I got drunk
there the first time, swam nude off the

lake-facing shore, turned down dares to swim
to the small island, short
as your boat. I circle both, rock shelves falling,
rising, that one lure behind me

like the forgotten wish to keep
finding you in kokanee and char.

Skin Diving Over the Shelf

Twenty yards out in one fathom, new sturgeon
long as my thumb skitter through green dust
and rubble from old slides. Then cutthroat fry

an arm's reach away. Then slowing down
until my breath in the tube and the slap
of wave on my ears makes one sound.

I never understand how letting go
makes the body float. Bay to my left,
open lake to right, I tune and point

north, waving my fins at the minimum
to keep me from sinking, never quite
a surrender. The growing and shrinking

whine of props, one by one, stitch industry
to noise and no-noise, but down below
an ancient sucker loved by nothing roams

out over the dark dropoff. It will destroy
every engine to make a home in one.
We will bring down the state if I follow it.

Lake Bottom

Tying up at Goose Island, she dove in, angled
down and over the mossy shelf of
granite and fry to the dropoff. She swam
with mackinaw into greener and greener
shade, and the belly spots of dolly varden

drew her down, pink coals. When she reached bottom
she could hear the glacier
still grinding south. Moraine fell all
around her onto the deepest
char and bull trout, onto the lost

reel and just flickering spoon, aspen leaf, can,
onto the belt of the murder victim,
aluminum slide. It rained and rained more stone
inside that icy ghost, and she lay down
hearing fire under silt, saw then her hands

work magic with the dark: bringing salmon
to birth from a fingertip, scything
the choker weeds, turning rubble into
food. Far above, the boat she came in
slipped from its knot around a ponderosa. Drifting

for two days, it broke up at last on the state beach.

Painted Rocks

Approach that bay by water, from the south,
leave Reservation air, leave three islands
back and pass a headland this map will say
screams, a bald eagle, Deweys Cove between

its beak. Pass in the quiet of that lie.
Or stop. Swallows angle down for the mouths
of their reflection, for gnats twirling green
like the old view of atoms. If tall granite

falls—a silent drop of crow, tamarack—
outlive its water-kiss, skirt guardian
salmon north along the smooth comb. If the rock wall stays,
pass bison small as a hand, pass the red hand

into your own holy air. One more bay
until the first one, those black wings folding back.

Fire Ring

We light bald, damp logs
with a propane torch. Rivers
keep flooding toward us

like buried gas, each tree stripped,
sown like loaves over the lake.

The Dock in Winter

spills itself out as the lake drops.
It gives up a lost wrench

from green moonslope already dry
by first snow. I walk

under ghost trails of perch
and the odd cutthroat. I make a circle

around all the shrinking beams.
I know I must drown this way,

over and over. I must die
and walk again, lean against the bone-white

crossbar watching the lake
freeze backward

into the Flathead and Lewis ranges,
all those mountains north into Glacier Park.

Orchard, April

She calls your name out mid-stroke
then slumps, each apple branch exploded
white a slow acre away.

Or she passes electric but dark,
veered off the word trail to your heart
—even now, the bark doubling.

Lookout on Miller Point

We reached the top with scrabble
in our shoes, with blood on the palms
that gripped the willow, pulled each
other up those last ten yards. There

we could see our wheezing selves.
We sat on a rock ledge and breathed
east, Table Bay behind us
and down, two hundred feet. And there

again the two islands, and two
miles out to river current,
log, salmon, and weed,
and another five to the east shore.

Thirty miles north and south. South wind,
an osprey diving. I pointed out
the winter cougar den
and lichen. You saw flintrock,

then Canada, all fifty-three
years from London to L.A.,
thirty more to that Point, inches
between us. I hold you there now,

keep us from risking our necks
on the way down. I held you to stone
even as we skidded
toward Doc Patterson's drive, the dark

of the woods what we limped through
home, your game knee and muscles
tightening, my limp because of yours
and because I grew up with you.

3.

Fraction Hymns and Sonnets out of Town

Shrinking

She gets up every day out of the ground
and garden rained on by her oldest grief,
her red-black tangle of petals so poison
they damage the eyes just to look. She

gets out of bed to find in the mirror
ribs and hips about to break out
of her skin, the face tight as a fist but
disappearing into eyes and the flat

mouth, everything shrinking like her small breasts
careless as waves of meringue, like her dark sex
where no one is ever allowed again.

On the phone at work, she chips at her mother
—useless bitch, 80 years old and still
got your head up your ass—chips until sparks
set fire to new abuse and ash

covers her desk like gray snow. She works it all
over and over into that soil
she comes back to, composting rage
and wreckage equally, the best of all

gardeners. There the last of her mother
restores the cineraria. Orchids
keep their heat all winter inside her,
even as the body pinches

its acid kingdom, shrinking like outer space
to her rescue or ruin, this weak sun
a kind of star she wants to live by.

That Year

The first tree, Chinese elm, made second base
and all the cheer of thousands, hovering high
and dark like shade. The first street ended dead
at the half circle of rhododendron.
You could smell the ocean ten miles away.
You could slide down the pitch of wild grass
to parking lot and grocery.

That year you first named evil, a man trolled
yard-to-yard for kids. A whole week, wildfire
spilled down the ridges, deer and puma stunned
by daylight neighborhoods. Evil found you,
a whisper in the loud skull. Ignored you
all through the rioting of August
worming its way toward a voice.

Georgic After an Argument

Leave me alone, love:
When I go down to the lake's edge, stay out
of my face as trout move,
slow to their welled-up anger—those flies loud

in their eyes, their skin
coming to surface in dark. Lay the words
on flagstone, ready as pine in the bin
to burn. Strike the match. Throw in the sore word.

I sleep on water tonight,
a wave a thought of leaving, then its kiss
on wet wood, then the tied
boat rocking. Wave after wave slap and miss

eroding more shore. Under this dock,
those muffled scenes in dream will flatten out.
And already you set the clock
that wakes the house at 6:00. We drive to town

talking again. I read your face,
the headlines, the road. Already we've pushed
our small country's flag of quiet
into a world that somehow will need us.

Already we must cut our throats
at the fury, the burning of other
lives. Die like trout rising to a city's hard dream,
rocked to black in the hold of this beggar.

Stocking Rock Creek

Each odd Friday, then, a rolling tank pulls
to the shoulder next to bridge. A man dips
a long-handled basket into boiling
trout, counts them through wire, waves the spraying wand

over creek. She learns to fish that way,
twenty yards downstream from miracle. How
different it is since, snagged in weed or stone
below a cutbank, each technique a failure,

Big Jack pouting. Even as it swims
away, she names it. And willow and pine
are salve, glove between her and a sprawling
desert. She might never hold that water ghost,

magic-wrecker, missing but visible
Christ. It noses away, into the real dark.

Self-Guided Tour to Avalanche Lake

The first hard frost, varied thrush song, ground
cracking in the green light of noon
and cedar bowing. Goatsbeard sways from a limb,
a face in that jagged face where a trunk
broke—stump of its body, crown far back

of its brain. There are no eyes here but hers.
The trail she walks on leads to bird call, trees
she's never heard of: the tips of hemlock
praising east, dwarf yew, and the mild clutch
of roots halving a stone. Down there, swirling of rock

grinds out potholes in the creek bed
falling down a gorge. The bridge she watches from
trembles. Water ouzel dip for insects
in the spray. And this is where the leaflet ends,
where name-stakes end, and wood that rises

to her right begins an unmarked climb.
At first, she knows her way by the furrowed
bark of cottonwood. A snowshoe rabbit track
points up. But then the five-pointed bract,
nine-note humming from a branch. And now

this darker walking, through the brittle white
on each leaf and chip. The trees thinning,
the air thinner and cold up there
where wild goats graze, she comes at last upon
the lake, the high curved walls of glaciers

sliding down. The shallow water here
froze weeks ago. Logs from unknown trees

glow gray beneath the ice, leaves held up
in their sinking. She chooses a rock,
skips it across the freeze. The sound now

of a bow let loose, quiver of air going out
in a strain for name that comes back on itself.

Two Days at Arch Cape

And the mild storm blew in, fraying the rim
of Hat Rock, and Neahkahnie Mountain
flew up its hundreds of feet over haystacks
and loaves and thumbs of calm, off-shore stone.

Inside the borrowed home, I let the wind
change, let lilies fill outside the window,
bow, empty, then fill again. I didn't
once think I didn't belong in my body,

or that I deserved a home this quiet
while outside, salal blooming even in stress,
a storm continued shifting speed, direction,
all clues the storm would have us find

about its nature there in the frightening,
judicious mixture I witnessed, unexplained.

Essay on Rime

I have seen the 200-year-old brick
of Maryland homes, and the pictograph

hovering on western granite. I have
passed the road in Idaho disappearing

under sand and blue sage. I have heard
Bishop Tutu claim we are all prisoners

of hope, I have known in my own jail
elms will fill the boulevards of heaven.

In every town, the wind flatters us.
Over the ground walk ants and ticks that could

poison our blood. Everything the wind
moves through makes a sound like words. Water talks,

the green rocks talk. It's not true that children
are wise, but they live and think about things

right here, and that's as solid as your hand,
real as its need to betray you.

In Nevada once, dust devils whirled away
from the center of a great silence. We

went to hear what sounded like nothing,
stood on the dry lakebed of the world to give

the son a drink of quiet, the daughter breath
without harm. We used to make the largest

noise here, deep under these feet, but now we've taken
it to every kind of street and called it poetry.

Man Burned for Spying

Before the stinging fire comes the air urged
up your shirt and across your cheek like spiders
of release. In the cracked thigh, your daughter
sings her adolescent rite. In the eye

swelling pointlessly, your son hears miles away
a heart stopping like a drum on the road
to factory. These last knives dart like
flames that won't cut in a fog of shuffling

heels and dust risen up to eye level.
That girl laughs at the spit on your arm.
Angry mouths burn to blur, to long queues
of missing teeth. They behold who they are

when what is not a scream begins.
They become one with the one they receive.

The Argument

Snow falling over hard snow,
one figure in that field hauls
all her color west, one storm
out of a heartscape of storm.

Her frontier opens his, whole
towns built on a prairie slow
to forgive any claim, all
these blank hills wanting to know.

Redwing

When we decided the river was God
and the cave her ringing tune, we stooped
to every roll of stampede, to all gray storm.
When we decided the river meant us
harm, the voice in redwood darkened too,
an ear in the gut blown to sandstone.

When we forgot evil, we forgot ourselves.
Walkers doubled, tripled as they crossed
the mall, rain washing each from the other.
We owned every bone. At night someone screamed
from the hut. We drove on, carried away
by dead populations as if shoved by a wave,

the fumbling hooves of talk, as if we were
the last redwing straddling the bison's hump.

After Being Quiet for a Long Time

You'd let the tongue wait longer. The slick road
heart-to-lip grow dangerous with weeds.
You'd stand at the open door watching earth
close a snowy mouth over each word.

A bell choir changed you. Squirrels in the attic.
The crying girl. A pencil breaking.
Where does all the noise go, going inside?
Waves slap and flatten on a cold lake.

After being quiet for a long time, you'd slip
over yourself toward talk, not at all
like you thought. You'd fall through anger and lust
as bad as always, the road without toll,

no bridges locked from here to either coast.
Someday again you'd think yourself through a meal,
biting through to silence. Quiet through dishes,
through sex or shower. Quiet through asking

or asking forgiveness. The larch, a dock,
your small boat would wait for you like the lake
for the first oar-pull into the middle,
for a word to say without breaking.

Violent Hours

He saw them coming in Needles, 114°.
They moved west from Chicago like desperate pioneers
mad to turn something over. He knew they lived
under sand and pavement, even in
fern he knelt in all those long afternoons
coming back to silence. The violent hours
overtook him through his heels like fever
every time he walked, every time
he had some place to go. They overtook him
like hot dream, less real
as the colors brightened. In time
he gave in to that swinging arm and flaming word,
angle of himself pressing
the kitchen table, polishing this loaded gun.

Suddenly it was the end of the century.
Cars looked mostly alike, and downtown buildings
curved and arched again, as in better days.
His children wanted to talk,
but he'd forgotten everything
but how to warn or teach: This is the best
shine of metal. A porch light goes on
for infinity. To be safe forever,
don't ask for much more. He took them
to the store and said down the long aisle
of vegetable and fruit, *See this, this is freedom,*
and he hardly walked fast to the car
sizzling in heat like some monster's dinner.

Where on earth would he find the split
second again without body-fear?
Where will blood slow as the wind comes inside,
the mind a shy follower? He drove home
along the coast, scared for himself,
for the father, for all his other names.
The violent hours found him again at a place
where west disappears,
and they moved in fast, a chattering storm
from the wrong directions,
there to supply all the arguments.

On the Train Across America in 1902

Their bodies rocked at night. Hills high as Scotland
leveled to grass long and tan, the lantern
swinging, jangling. The two children talked in their
sleeps. Her husband shrunk inside his coat while she

saw dark change to dawn and smoke and the wide
river at St. Louis. West of there,
the great rise and the sod house, post hole
and rattlesnake, and each time a storm

walked down the plain toward Greeley, the smell
of horses and drying jerky. She made that
rain's wind into music, and she moved to it
those ten years after the Ghost Dance, the Lakota-

Celtic tune about land and being cleared from it,
the dust as rain fell about rising again.

Moon in Smoke, Teton Park

We waited until you carved
the yellow darkness out, moved

land away like one still loved
but a burden—pulling up

in light you owned, did not own,
as wind exploded, as green

flared to red in praise of you,
circling, bringing back the dark seed.

How November Comes

Open a door for them and the graybacks
fly out whatever thigh or arm the light
hits first. This is how the season puts on
its clothes and the undescribed heart of you
falls away, pieces for the coming cold.

Funny how the sound you make from far off
is the same sound the small muscle makes,
tuning. You could fool yourself into thinking
you breathed two places at once when sky,
a sudden red, filled with leaving geese

familiar as blood, and the sky the next
morning, clouded now, filled with nothing more
wonderful than tricky wind and its partner
sparrows, long days ahead without sun.

Sign

I once lived in a valley of victims.
A man who'd lost his arm to a thresher
tucked the empty sleeve into itself
like a new kind of blossom and passed by.
He smiled at me, glad in the secret of wound.
With his one arm he waved
to the scalpless woman, the leprous grandfather,
the boy of mine born without a tongue.

I used to wonder if the water
rearranged us for defeat. I noticed,
those few times out of town, others running
headlong and firm, as if the bad were not
right in front of them. I noticed
laughter unfrightened by the corner ahead
or the dark, swirling pool. In my valley
the drowned come back to us in all their wet clothes.
They go house to house singing on the lawns,
begging for jackets, a single embrace.

I left the day our daughter, bleeding from the ear,
led us upstream, into a narrow range.
We found animals indifferent and harmless.
We found humans with all their limbs
and faculties. Though I am not sure,
I believe evil follows gravity,
grace brims through ever thinning layers
of air. I will never again lead my family
to a place so low we rejoice in what disappears.
I will live uncertainly without disease
or verdict. I will teach my son
the sign for tomorrow.

Pictures

They came home whole, mostly, still for war
but glad to be done with it. Spouses ran
across tarmacs hour by hour, broadcast live
as pairs embraced, kissed long, hard, their children
stuck like gum to one thigh or another.

Losers made it home for civil war
on foot. Stunned by hunger, by life, they ran
to kabob stand and street corner alive
with resent. They broke bread with wife and children.
They hid their guns, fed on one another.

These are the pictures we remember most.
Not fear of gas or anthrax. Not half-lost
shuffling from deadline to bomb. When blackout
comes again, in town or mind, we keep count
of each afterimage pulled toward absence,

each carnation missing dawn after dawn
from a kitchen bouquet. Those scenes go on
without our eyes, like the best parts of books.
Loud pages of grace and knives kiss hard in oak.
They hide from the bare table of sense.

Lockerbie

Down and behind, a pop blossoms like wind
slapping your fragile ears, then all heaven's
angels keep your heart beating
even as it's pressed into the seatback.
Angels soften the breathless, unbelieving
cry at the angle and the new roaring.

Most of us will sleep until you kiss us
deep in our beds. Brown brick falls in our chests
red with fire, the second thought of you.
I wonder about this nightmare rain.
As long as I breathe, I hate these scuffed stones
where metal comes to rest. I hate your dull

thudding pasture to pasture like sick jokes
breaking the backs of our sheep. I hate you,
bastards, for living through the long dark air,
down through the sound of Aunt Elsie's prayer,
William's dirty song with the boys,
Bob and Lucy's rough lovemaking, my son's

dreamy laugh, living all that way down
in a jelly smoke so one or two of you
can whisper before you die,
Help us. It wasn't our fault.
As the red flashing world races our way,
I hear the quiet inside my breath

and give it back to the dirt. I live
to tell you this story, but like a priest
I break the bread over and over
and the blood is nowhere. The sacrifice
moves to other towns every second,
moving and unmoving each life.

Confession

At the foot of the mountain, day by day,
a woodpecker dismantled our house. These hands
I used to rub the necks of wife and sons
turned hard and cold. I knew a dream losing
its blood. At the ballpark, dust puffed up
from the bag full of resin and resolve
as snow began to fall. The wind here quit,
then sky trailed behind. It went its own way.

Or did I never reach that first makeshift rise?
Was I crippled by the dead well in Illinois,
driven mad by cranes along the Platte?
In the east-moving wash of air
black qualms arrived like willing fish. Did I
swim back with them? Did I murder their eyes?

After the Miracle

A gate in the spine open, muscles there
gone slack as clothesline, finally and now
strangely her back doesn't exist, the pain
swept away as cleanly as the factory's

acid air once the wind shifts. She sits,
remembering tightness, the way it drew
all of her to its center, distracting
any motion, any other thought. After

the miracle, after the all of her
focused inward suddenly disappeared,
what was there left but doubt in the new walk
and restored axis? Fearing ease, braced

for the wrong step that would freeze her to her
spasm—come home again, familiar—
what were the yard and house but background again
to inward attention, this time on absence,

on the emptiness of her without pain,
while the dumb flesh spread out, and body hair
twisted toward light, and grass filled the yard,
and lawn, trees, and gate opened to the street?

Our Empty House

We stop imagining you when that eclipse,
three minutes of dark between roiling shade,
leaps through our skin to turn the bones black.
Our kitchen stays warm those bright days I pray

the phone will stop ringing. It ends with a wrong
number, then cursing. Then a hum grows
loud toward fall until the furnace growls
in envy and we turn that off. We know,

carrying the dead with us, letting them
leak into our future, into your birth—
we know you can only choose to hate us
like a tide of poison staining shorebirds

crippled past any real music. We know
that helpless sound. It fooled us once, too.

Demonstration

I never told you about Tonopah,
100° into the Mojave, the Mizpah Hotel
my grandfather and I stayed at
blurring in red-brick waves, the slot machines
clutching and rolling. I knew Boron,
town of the dead coyote, lay up the road.
I knew I'd have my last meal there
before crawling lower than sage, just above snakes
toward the flat basin and the one plywood shack
trimmed with single-rod antennas.
I never told you I was there when circles flew outward
on the sand, when that shack sunk ten feet
into desert floor, a huge cake suddenly collapsed.
I never told you I lay on my stomach
at the edge of the explosion,
swimming in shock waves, riding a roar
still traveling in every direction of space.
When I saw the shack disappear, when I saw bolts
of lighting ground-to-cloud and, sideways,
hill-to-hill, I knew I could never
look right at you again, nor even Pop
in his room back in town 30 years before.
In our home 1000 miles east, you were teaching
our youngest to talk. I drove back to you
on the other side of speech,
practicing a way to blow memory back together,
rehearsing the way to meet your eyes
without our skulls showing.

The Heavens

With the help of the Hubble telescope,
astrophysicists have calculated the age of the
universe to be younger than many of the
bodies within it.
—News item

If you're 41 and always tired,
even as the soul, the urge to screw
spin away like gauzy twisters
from your wrecked town, the impossible's not so hard
to believe. Long ago I found day and air
turning in that dark surf at rip. The angel
once whispered me home. And now the body
ages faster than the theme of itself,
the forest white pines older
than the forest.

Certainly we've twirled
longer on our own than this brief orbit
tonight, together, blazing through
even younger space. Certainly I grow new
the more outward I go, forward
and farther into every other life—
At last I'm the pulsing satellite
near and around each worldly thing, younger
than my birth, an umbrella above all
possible rains, humming large as the one
great idea.

Or no: I never lived.
Dead from the start, my legs twitch and I call

the motion dancing. Or I
never danced. It's only this closed circuit of turns
leaning back toward simple chalk lines.

It meant something once to hear a voice
reaching across the river. Maybe heaven
called, maybe another being
leaking out of itself. The moment the universe
explodes from its compact darkness,
you make the sign. Now that God only whispers,
it's up to you to look back, winking, letting go
of the pull of that tenth orbit, a small
wobbling toward the end, the beginning, of time.

The Lunar Driver

Sage connects to lava rock mile by mile.
West of Atomic City, blue flowers
in the craters of the moon. Jackrabbits
now where the sheep kill was. Road following
wind. Handsful of grass. The blue wind. The black.

Lyndon Johnson stood here for the roadside
plaque, Arco still in flames. The Big Lost
and Little Lost rivers disappeared into
their own sinks, ten miles apart, at the Idaho
National Lab. And thousands come home

to their roads like clouds. And any given
dead one, bird or girl, might circle this place
missing life, backing off the plateau
into sky, letting go of one green wheel.

Bread

The day we heard about her cancer,
the kind in the brain and lungs, whatever that means,
the longest cold spell of winter slipped
away like short-term memory, now to the surface
and quietly over a set of falls, down
to a river silent and out of view. Each warmer day
dazed us with sun: My wife shoveled her walk
five doors west, I made them potato rolls,
and among women a chain of prayer
extended all over town. Looking for my friend,
I wanted to touch him on the shoulder, that gateway
to another grief, just to ask what
he needed. I thought only of that exchange,
what I would say not to fumble, and I guessed
his jaded, grateful answer. I guessed
the humor there.

But it never worked that way:
Both of them simply disappeared
into the shrinking of tumors,
into managing pain, that escape in slow drives
between city and town that took them
by cow fields, brick barns,
any reminder of France. She was cold and hot
all at once those days, so they'd fidget
with the fan all the way back from the doctor's,
tires on wet road like bacon sizzling, my friend
asleep a lot of the time. When they talked
it was not like in the movies. I now know
this all third-hand, and what you need to understand
is that in two months she went
from fear to desire, he from fear to love.

They let go into loneliness knowing
it part of the orbit.

                                        I only found this out
later. What I did those months was find signs
everywhere: in the weather, the start of Lent,
my cough, every gesture of hers
before I'd heard, the air, the soil.
On Ash Wednesday evening, the church was her body
we lived and sang to fill. Black pressed
the stain out of glass. I ate
and drank from her, our mutual sacrifice.
There are times in your life when you feel
inside great unspeakable mystery.
It makes you tremble. That is the sign.
There are other times, growing your own grief,
when you force an utter
sense on the world. I never cared for her
the way I thought I did. She left my galaxy,
my river with its talking stones. Am I
unkind to say this? I am. I talk
like someone who will die alone.

I don't really know desire, or love, the roles
for leavers and stayers. Every time
that lake comes back in memory, though,
the ice long gone, the sun high, hot,
salmon biting at any color or flash,
the world composes itself exponentially
around the meal appearing as I say it
on picnic tables at the end of this
great day. Everyone I've ever cared for
is here. We complain about the hornets.
We wonder about the cold breeze out of Canada.
And all of us praise the fish, the whole spread
two grandparents made because feeding

the hungry is what it's always all about. No one
has died yet, although I know they will.
They are feeding us, even as they leave.
They are inside of us, kneeling and singing.
They break us and tear from within
as if we were bread. They help us
turn new into the life we didn't know was already here.

Acknowledgments

Some of the poems in this collection appeared first in the following publications:

Anthology of Magazine Verse and Yearbook of American Poetry: "After the Miracle," "May on the Wintered-Over Ground"
Chariton Review: "Roethke on Film"
Colorado Review: "Lake Bottom"
Gravity's Loophole: "Crossing the Arctic Waste with Ana," "Lockerbie," "Mansface," "Paparazzo," "Shrinking," "That Year"
Great River Review: "On the Train Across America in 1902"
The Helena Review: "The High Lake Past the Field"
Hubbub: "Dick," "The Lunar Driver"
Indiana Review: "Georgic After an Argument"
Interim: "The Bulldog Edition of *The Los Angeles Times*"
Kinesis: "By Moonlight," "Douglas Islands"
Mankato Poetry Review: "The Lunar Driver"
Manoa: "After Being Quiet for a Long Time"
Mid-American Review: "How November Comes"
MSU Humanities Connection: "The Argument"
The Nebraska Review: "Lookout on Miller Point"
The North American Review: "After the Miracle," "Coming Back to Life," "May on the Wintered-Over Ground"
Ordinary Time: "Meditation"
Pacific Poetry and Fiction Review: "Self-Guided Tour to Avalanche Lake"
Poetry Northwest: "George McGovern Campaign Rally, San Diego, 1972," "Lon Chaney, Jr., at the Supermarket in Capistrano Beach"
Poetry 2000 Poetry Desk Calendar: "Moon in Smoke, Teton Park"
The Seattle Review: "Two Days at Arch Cape"
Talking River Review: "The Heavens," "Rosary"
Third Coast: "Demonstration"
Two Cities: "On Not Introducing Myself to the Poet Laureate When We Both Shopped for Art at the Phillips Gallery, Salt Lake City," "Stocking Rock Creek"

Many thanks to the Mankato State University Research Committee, the Region Nine and Prairie Lakes Regional Arts councils, the McKnight Foundation, and the National Endowment for the Arts for encouragement and financial support during the time these poems were written.

Note on section 3: "Fraction hymns" are sung at the breaking of the bread during a Christian liturgy.

About the Author

Richard Robbins grew up in California and Montana. His first collection, *The Invisible Wedding*, was published in 1984. Over the years, Robbins has received awards from the Minnesota State Arts Board, Hawthornden Castle International Retreat for Writers, the McKnight Foundation and the National Endowment for the Arts. He currently directs the creative writing program and the Good Thunder Reading Series at Minnesota State University, and lives in Mankato with his wife, the poet Candace Black, and their two sons.